WHAT
ARE THE
LUTHERAN
CONFESSIONS?

CONCORDIA PUBLISHING HOUSE · SAINT LOUIS

1 2 3 4 5 6 7 8 9 10   31 30 29 28 27 26 25 24 23 22

ABBREVIATIONS

AC	Augsburg Confession
Ap	Apology of the Augsburg Confession
Ep	Epitome of the Formula of Concord
FC	Formula of Concord
LC	Large Catechism
SA	Smalcald Articles
SC	Small Catechism
SD	Solid Declaration of the Formula of Concord
Tr	Treatise on the Power and Primacy of the Pope

CITATION EXAMPLES

AC XX 4	Augsburg Confession, Article XX, paragraph 4
Ap IV 229	Apology of the AC, Article IV, paragraph 229
FC SD X 24	Solid Declaration of the Formula of Concord, Article X, paragraph 24
FC Ep V 8	Epitome of the Formula of Concord, Article V, paragraph 8
LC V 32, 37	Large Catechism, Part 5, paragraphs 32 and 37
SA III I 6	Smalcald Articles, Part III, Article I, paragraph 6
SC III 5	Small Catechism, Part III, paragraph 5
Tr 5	Treatise, paragraph 5

INTRODUCTION

After the Bible, the Lutheran Church holds the Book of Concord as the standard of doctrine, life, and practice for Lutheran congregations. In turn, Lutheran congregations are identified as those who believe, teach, and confess the truths of God's Word as they are summarized and confessed in the Book of Concord. When a pastor is ordained, or set aside for his office, he promises that he will perform his pastoral duties in accord with the Lutheran Confessions. Other workers in the Lutheran Church—like Lutheran teachers, directors of Christian education, deaconesses, and directors of parish music—also promise that they will perform their duties in accord with the Lutheran Confessions. When men and women are confirmed in the Lutheran Church, they are asked if they confess the doctrine of the Evangelical Lutheran Church as they have learned to know it from the Small Catechism to be faithful and true. Since the days of the Reformation, this handful of key documents has been the core teaching of those who call themselves Lutherans. This collection grew out of the need to clearly state and defend the faith founded in Jesus Christ as revealed in Scripture.

> Being instructed from the prophetic and apostolic Scriptures, we are sure about our doctrine and Confession. (Preface to the Book of Concord, paragraph 22)

The Lutheran Confessions are the ten documents gathered together in the Book of Concord, which was first published in

1580. Some of these documents are formal statements presented to government and religious officials. Two of the documents are catechisms, which were written to teach the faith to all ages. Some of these Confessions were written by Martin Luther; others were written by his colleague Philip Melanchthon. The Formula of Concord, the last document in the Lutheran Confessions, is from the 1570s and was crafted specifically to address controversies that arose after Luther's death. All of these statements summarize and confess the truths of God's Word. The Book of Concord still unites Lutherans as a common confession of faith. This booklet will introduce you to these important treasures from the Reformation. The summaries in this booklet only skim the surface of the Lutheran Confessions. When you are finished with this booklet, you should be better prepared to delve into the rich depths of the truth of God's Word in the Confessions themselves.

Note: In the outlines of each of the documents, sometimes square brackets are used to indicate different headings that were not original to the Book of Concord. These were included in the edition titled Concordia: The Lutheran Confessions *for clarity and reference use. Not all the headings in the outline have summaries in the overview of the Book of Concord. Due to space limitations, some sections of certain documents were given less summary space than others. All the headings were included nonetheless so that you could better understand the structure of the Book of Concord. If you would like to know more about certain sections, we encourage you to find them in* Concordia: The Lutheran Confessions.

NAME	DATE	AUTHOR	SUMMARY
Apostles' Creed	Second Century	Unknown	Baptismal Creed used in Rome.
Nicene Creed	325, 381	Assembled church leaders at the Council of Nicaea (325) and the Council of Constantinople	Creed intended to clearly state, on the basis of Scripture, that Jesus Christ is true God, equal with the Father, and that the Holy Spirit is also true God, equal with the Father and the Son.
Athanasian Creed	Sixth–Eighth Centuries	Unknown; named after the great Church Father Athanasius, who was instrumental in the drafting of the Nicene Creed	Confession of the teaching of the Trinity and the person and work of Jesus Christ.
Small Catechism	1529	Martin Luther	A short work that was to educate the laity in the basics of the Christian faith.
Large Catechism	1529	Martin Luther	A series of re-edited sermons of Luther that cover the same chief parts of Christian doctrine as the Small Catechism.

NAME	DATE	AUTHOR	SUMMARY
Augsburg Confession	June 25, 1530	Philip Melanchthon	The chief Lutheran Confession, which was presented by the earliest Lutherans to Emperor Charles V at the Imperial Diet of Augsburg as a statement of the chief articles of the Christian faith as understood by Lutherans; also contains a listing of abuses that the Lutherans had corrected.
Apology of the Augsburg Confession	May 1531	Philip Melanchthon	A lengthy defense authored by Melanchthon after the Roman theologians had condemned many of the teachings of the Augsburg Confession; rightly considered a Christian classic.

NAME	DATE	AUTHOR	SUMMARY
Smalcald Articles	1536	Martin Luther	Articles of faith intended by Luther to be an ecumenical platform for an upcoming Church council; stated what the Lutherans could not compromise and why.
Treatise on the Power and Primacy of the Pope	1537	Philip Melanchthon	A supplement to the Augsburg Confession that gives the Lutheran position on the pope.
Formula of Concord	1577	Jacob Andreae, Martin Chemnitz, Nicholas Selnecker	A restatement of some teachings in the Augsburg Confession over which Lutherans had become divided. The Solid Declaration is the unabridged version. The Epitome is an abridged version intended for congregations to study. More than 8,100 pastors and theologians signed it, as well as more than 50 government leaders.

Note: The documents in the chart are listed in chronological order of when they were written rather than the order they can be found in the Book of Concord.

THE THREE UNIVERSAL OR ECUMENICAL CREEDS

Lutheranism is not a new faith, but a continuation of the historic, Christian faith. With Christians of all times, and in all places, we confess what God's Word teaches—nothing more, and nothing less. A creed is a formal statement of faith, and the three universal or ecumenical creeds are summary statements Christians have agreed on for centuries. Lutheranism does not regard the traditions and teachings of Christians who have gone before as equal to Scripture. Instead, the creeds summarize the truth of Scripture, especially about who God is and what God does for us. The most ancient of all Confessions of faith used by Lutherans are the Apostles' Creed, the Nicene Creed, and the Athanasian Creed.

THE APOSTLES' CREED

The Apostles' Creed was not written by the apostles but is a faithful summary of the teachings of the apostles as found in the Bible. Composed sometime in the second century, it is a continuation of an earlier creed Christians used in Rome. The wording of the Creed, as we confess it today, can be traced to southern Gaul (France).

THE NICENE CREED

The Nicene Creed is spoken today in many Lutheran congregations during Communion services or Church festivals. It was written during the First Council of Nicaea (AD 325) and revised by the First Council of Constantinople (AD 381). One addition to the original formula—that the Holy Spirit proceeds from the Father "and the Son"—comes from the Western tradition of the Church and appears as early as the Third Council (Synod) of Toledo (AD 589).

THE ATHANASIAN CREED

The Athanasian Creed is the longest of the three universal creeds. It is included in Lutheran hymnals, but many congregations read it publicly only on Trinity Sunday (the First Sunday after Pentecost). It is named after Athanasius, the great fourth-century champion of the truth of God's Word against those who denied that Jesus is God. The creed originated in southern Gaul (France), probably about the middle of the sixth century. The inclusion of the three ancient creeds in the Book of Concord shows that Lutherans are not a splinter group but that they embrace and confess the ancient faith of the Church.

THE AUGSBURG CONFESSION

Philip Melanchthon wrote the Augsburg Confession in 1530. Emperor Charles V of the Holy Roman Empire had invited Lutheran princes and theologians to attend a meeting of government leaders at the town of Augsburg. He wanted to discuss how the religious controversy in his empire could be settled. The emperor desired that German Lutheran princes would join the imperial forces to keep the invading armies of the Ottoman Turks out of Europe. At this meeting, the German Lutheran princes presented the emperor with the Augsburg Confession. The Augsburg Confession is composed from several documents that had already existed but were combined by Melanchthon to give a clear but conciliatory summary of the teachings and practices of the Lutheran pastors and congregations. To this day, it is the basic Lutheran Confession.

OUTLINE

Preface to Emperor Charles V	XVI. Civil Government
I. God	XVII. Christ's Return for Judgment
II. Original Sin	XVIII. Free Will
III. The Son of God	XIX. The Cause of Sin
IV. Justification	XX. Good Works
V. The Ministry	XXI. Worship of the Saints
VI. New Obedience	A Summary Statement
VII. The Church	A Review of the Various Abuses That Have Been Corrected
VIII. What the Church Is	XXII. Both Kinds in the Sacrament
IX. Baptism	XXIII. The Marriage of Priests
X. The Lord's Supper	XXIV. The Mass
XI. Confession	XXV. Confession
XII. Repentance	XXVI. The Distinction of Meats
XIII. The Use of the Sacraments	XXVII. Monastic Vows
XIV. Order in the Church	XXVIII. Church Authority
XV. Church Ceremonies	Conclusion

ARTICLE I. GOD

This article confesses that God is one divine essence in three distinct persons—Father, Son, and Holy Spirit. The Scriptures reveal this great mystery, confessed by all faithful Christians throughout time.

ARTICLE II. ORIGINAL SIN

Sin is a terminal disease. We are all conceived and born in sin; we inherit it from our first parents, Adam and Eve. The disease of sin can be overcome, but only by one medicine: the cleansing, healing, and forgiving blood of God's own Son.

ARTICLE III. THE SON OF GOD

Many early controversies about Christ's human and divine natures were resolved through careful study of God's Word and are reflected in the Nicene Creed. This article echoes that creed—our Lord Jesus Christ is one person who has two natures. He is both truly God and truly man.

ARTICLE IV. JUSTIFICATION

There is a historic saying in Lutheranism that the Church stands or falls on the article of justification. To justify means "to declare righteous." God's sure and certain declaration that we are righteous in His eyes is possible only because of our Savior, Jesus Christ.

> Our churches teach that people cannot be justified before God by their own strength, merits, or works. People are freely justified for Christ's sake, through faith, when they believe that they are received into favor and that their sins are forgiven for Christ's sake. By His death, Christ made satisfaction for our

sins. God counts this faith for righteousness in His sight (Romans 3 and 4). (AC IV)

ARTICLE V. THE MINISTRY

How can what Christ did for us two thousand years ago be effective in our lives today? The Holy Spirit works through ministers to distribute the Means of Grace, God's Word and Sacraments. Through these, we receive justification by grace alone, through faith alone, on account of Christ alone.

> Through the Word and Sacraments, as through instruments, the Holy Spirit is given. He works faith, when and where it pleases God, in those who hear the good news that God justifies those who believe that they are received into grace for Christ's sake. This happens not through our own merits, but for Christ's sake. (AC V 2–3)

ARTICLE VI. NEW OBEDIENCE

People sometimes accuse Lutherans of denying that Christians should do good works. This article clearly states that Lutherans do insist on good works. Good works do not save us. They are always the result of saving faith.

ARTICLE VII. THE CHURCH

Many of the reasons for the Reformation revolved around the clutter of man-made ceremonies that had accumulated by the sixteenth century. Article VII focuses on the very heart of the matter of the Reformation and defines church with beautiful simplicity.

> Our churches teach that one holy Church is to remain forever. The Church is the congregation of

saints in which the Gospel is purely taught and the Sacraments are correctly administered. (AC VII 1)

ARTICLE VIII. WHAT THE CHURCH IS

This article elaborates on Article VII and helps clarify what the Church is. The Church consists only of believers in Christ, people who are made holy by His mercy. The Church exists wherever the Word is proclaimed and the Sacraments are properly administered, even if by evil men.

ARTICLE IX. BAPTISM

The Bible teaches that Baptism is a gift of God's grace by which He applies the benefits of Christ's life, death, and resurrection to us personally. Because Baptism is God's way of bringing us salvation, infants should also be baptized.

> Our churches condemn the Anabaptists, who reject the Baptism of children, and say that children are saved without Baptism. (AC IX 3)

ARTICLE X. THE LORD'S SUPPER

By the time of the Augsburg Confession, deep divisions had arisen among the various reformers concerning the Lord's Supper. Lutherans believe, teach, and confess that, as Christ said of the bread, "This is My body," and of the wine, "This is My blood." These are given and shed "for the forgiveness of sins."

> Our churches teach that the body and blood of Christ are truly present and distributed to those who eat the Lord's Supper. They reject those who teach otherwise. (AC X)

ARTICLE XI. CONFESSION

The problem addressed by this article is that the Roman Catholic Church demanded every sin be recalled and confessed during times of private Confession and Absolution. This, however, is humanly impossible and makes our forgiveness dependent on our work and not on Christ.

ARTICLE XII. REPENTANCE

The Roman Catholic teaching about repentance was the spark that ignited the Lutheran Reformation. Repentance is not about "paying off" God or making up to God for our sin through good works. Repentance is recognizing the reality of our sin and turning to God in faith for His mercy.

ARTICLE XIII. THE USE OF THE SACRAMENTS

God gives the Sacraments—Baptism and the Lord's Supper—to His people for their forgiveness, life, and salvation. God attaches His Word of promise to the element of the Sacrament—water, wine, or bread—and gives and strengthens the faith of those receiving them.

ARTICLE XIV. ORDER IN THE CHURCH

This article defends the proper way to call pastors, that is, the Church's historic practice of placing personally and theologically qualified men into the office of preaching and teaching the Gospel and administering the Sacraments.

ARTICLE XV. CHURCH CEREMONIES

Lutheranism embraces the good historic traditions of the Church, such as following the pattern of the Church Year and a liturgical order of worship. Lutherans use these things to focus on Christ and to follow good order in the Church, never to earn the forgiveness of sins.

Our churches teach that ceremonies ought to be observed that may be observed without sin. Also, ceremonies and other practices that are profitable for tranquility and good order in the Church (in particular, holy days, festivals, and the like) ought to be observed. (AC XV 1)

ARTICLE XVI. CIVIL GOVERNMENT

This article points to the biblical doctrine of the two kingdoms. This is a way of speaking about God's care for us both spiritually through the Church and in earthly things through various orders in society, mainly through households and the government.

ARTICLE XVII. CHRIST'S RETURN FOR JUDGMENT

This article affirms the biblical view of the end times. It rejects any speculation or opinion about believers ruling the world before the final resurrection of the dead, as many people have falsely interpreted.

ARTICLE XVIII. FREE WILL

Apart from God's grace, we are wholly incapable of perceiving spiritual things. In worldly matters, we do have the freedom to make decisions according to human reason. In matters of eternal life, God gives us Christ's perfect righteousness as a gift by His Spirit working through His Word.

Our churches teach that a person's will has some freedom to choose civil righteousness and to do things subject to reason. It has no power, without the Holy Spirit, to work the righteousness of God, that is, spiritual righteousness. . . . Our churches condemn the Pelagians and others who teach that

17

without the Holy Spirit, by natural power alone, we are able to love God above all things and do God's commandments according to the letter. (AC XVIII 1–2, 8–9)

ARTICLE XIX. THE CAUSE OF SIN

The blame for sin rests solely with the devil and with us, not with God. Apart from God's mercy in Christ, there is no hope for sinners. Sin is a deep corruption of that which God created and is entirely mankind's fault.

ARTICLE XX. GOOD WORKS

This article lays out the Bible's clear teaching that good works are the fruit of faith, not the cause of our salvation. The Augsburg Confession asserts very clearly that our good works are necessary not to earn eternal life but because this is God's desire for our lives.

> Furthermore, we teach that it is necessary to do good works. This does not mean that we merit grace by doing good works, but because it is God's will. It is only by faith, and nothing else, that forgiveness of sins is apprehended. The Holy Spirit is received through faith, hearts are renewed and given new affections, and then they are able to bring forth good works. (AC XX 27–29)

ARTICLE XXI. WORSHIP OF THE SAINTS

Deep corruption had developed within the Roman Catholic Church regarding the honor given to the saints, resulting in what could only be described as false worship. This article disproves this false practice of praying to the saints that had arisen.

ARTICLE XXII. BOTH KINDS IN THE SACRAMENT

Prior to the Reformation, the practice had developed of withholding the consecrated wine from the common people during the Lord's Supper. Using Scripture, this article discredits this practice and points the Church to give both the bread and the wine to all participants in the Lord's Supper.

> The laity are given both kinds in the Sacrament of the Lord's Supper because this practice has the Lord's command, "Drink of it, all of you" (Matthew 26:27). (AC XXII 1–2)

ARTICLE XXIII. THE MARRIAGE OF PRIESTS

At the time of the Reformation, the Roman Catholic Church had made an unscriptural decree that forbade priests from marrying. The Lutherans maintained that the Church has no authority from God to command what He has not commanded, nor to forbid what He has not forbidden.

ARTICLE XXIV. THE MASS

Among many other good historic worship practices of the Church, Lutheranism retained the traditional form of the Mass, that is, the service of Holy Communion. Christ gave the Church this Sacrament as a gift and a blessing, to be used in faith by the people of God.

ARTICLE XXV. CONFESSION

During the first two centuries of Lutheran history, private Confession and Absolution between a pastor and a Church member was not abandoned. What the Lutheran Reformation corrected were the false teachings about Confession: that through certain activities people could make up for their sins. We are forgiven by grace through faith in Christ, not by our works.

ARTICLE XXVI. THE DISTINCTION OF MEATS

By the time of the Reformation, the Roman Catholic Church had devised complex regulations commanding Christians to avoid certain foods on certain days. This article corrects this false teaching while still approving practices that are beneficial for holding up the Gospel.

ARTICLE XXVII. MONASTIC VOWS

During the Middle Ages, many common people believed that only priests, monks, and nuns were truly performing spiritual work. This article lifts up such biblical duties as being a faithful husband, wife, son, or daughter, and takes great care to reject the harmful practice of monasticism.

ARTICLE XXVIII. CHURCH AUTHORITY

Over the course of centuries, Roman Catholic bishops had become not merely Church leaders but political figures as well. By returning to a biblical understanding of Church, this article clarifies that the true authority of Church leaders is in spiritual, not political, matters.

৪০৬৪

The Apology of the Augsburg Confession

After the Augsburg Confession had been read to the emperor, a committee of Roman Catholic theologians prepared a reply called the Confutation. This Confutation sent the message that the Roman Catholics did not agree with the Augsburg Confession and that the Lutherans had to back down or suffer punishment. It was read aloud to Lutheran leaders. The Lutherans were never given a copy of the document but were ordered to accept all its conclusions, make no reply to it, and not allow it to be published. Some who heard the Confutation, however, wrote it down word for word so the Lutheran leaders would know what it said. The Apology, written in 1531 by Philip Melanchthon, defends the Augsburg Confession against the accusations of the Confutation.

OUTLINE

Note: The outline for the Apology, or "defense," of the Augsburg Confession has two sets of numbers. Neither set is fully in order because of the way Melanchthon responded to the issues presented by the Confutation. The first set of numbers correspond to the article numbers of the Augsburg Confession; the parenthetical numbers correspond to the original Apology.

Greeting	[Passages the Adversaries Misuse]
I. God	[The Adversaries' Teaching Based on Reason and the Law]
II (I). Original Sin	[Results of the Adversaries' Teaching]
III. Christ	[Salvation Is by God's Mercy]
IV (II). Justification	[The Adversaries' Other Arguments]
What Is Justifying Faith?	[Conclusion]
Faith in Christ Justifies	VII and VIII (IV). The Church
We Obtain Forgiveness of Sins through Faith Alone in Christ	IX. Baptism
[Scripture Affirms This Teaching]	X. The Holy Supper
[The Church Fathers Affirm This Teaching]	XI. Confession
[The Adversaries Reject This Teaching]	XIIa (V). Repentance
V (III). Love and Fulfilling the Law	[The Two Parts of Repentance]
[No One Can Keep the Law Perfectly]	[Scriptural Proofs]
[Church Fathers and St. Paul Affirm Justification through Faith]	[Forgiveness of Sins Received by Faith]
Reply to the Adversaries' Arguments	[Faith and Repentance]

XIIb (VI). Confession and Satisfaction	XXI (IX). The Invocation of Saints
[The Church Fathers on Satisfaction]	XXII (X). Both Kinds in the Lord's Supper
[Misuses of Scripture]	XXIII (XI). The Marriage of Priests
[Additional False Teachings]	[Arguments for the Marriage of Priests]
[True Repentance Produces Good Works]	[Conclusion]
XIII (VII). The Number and Use of the Sacraments	XXIV (XII). The Mass
XIV. Order in the Church	What Is a Sacrifice, The Kinds of Sacrifice
XV (VIII). Human Traditions in the Church	What the Fathers Thought about Sacrifice
XVI. Political Order	The Use of the Sacrament and of the Sacrifice
XVII. Christ's Return for Judgment	The Term *Mass*
XVIII. Free Will	[The Mass for the Dead]
XIX. The Cause of Sin	XXVII (XIII). Monastic Vows
XX. Good Works	XXVIII (XIV). Church Authority

ARTICLE I. GOD

Lutherans clearly identify themselves with the Church of all times and places by confessing the biblical teaching of the Holy Trinity. Lutherans also reject the teachings of all those who deny the one true God: Father, Son, and Holy Spirit.

ARTICLE II (I). ORIGINAL SIN

By the sixteenth century, Roman Catholic theologians had come to view original sin as only a weakness in human nature. The Scriptures, as the Lutherans and Church Fathers argued, teach instead that original sin is the absence of original righteousness, or goodness in our natures, and is the root cause of all sin.

> The ancient definition of original sin is that it is a lack of righteousness. This definition not only denies that mankind is capable of obedience in his body, but also denies that mankind is capable of knowing God, placing confidence in God, fearing and loving God, and certainly also the ability to produce such things. (Ap II 23)

ARTICLE III. CHRIST

It was very important for the Lutherans to affirm the historic biblical teaching of the Church: Christ is fully God and fully man. The next article, on justification, is rooted in this article on Christ.

ARTICLE IV (II). JUSTIFICATION

Article IV of the Apology is the most complex and detailed article in the entire Book of Concord. Because it deals with our salvation, how God has forgiven our sins and has reconciled us to Himself in Christ, it is also the most important. It is the very heart of the Gospel.

> By their own strength, people cannot fulfill God's Law. They are all under sin, subject to eternal wrath and death. Because of this, we cannot be freed by the Law from sin and be justified. But the promise of forgiveness of sins and of justification has been given us for Christ's sake, who was given for us in order that He might make satisfaction for the sins of the world. (Ap IV 40)

ARTICLE V (III). LOVE AND FULFILLING THE LAW

Over time, the Roman Catholic Church had confused the distinction between the effects of God's Law on people before and after their justification. This had disastrous consequences. Melanchthon returns to the consequences for this false teaching constantly, writing the longest article in the Apology in order to clarify this distinction.

> Because of His promise, God wishes to be gracious and to justify for Christ's sake, not because of the Law or our works. (Ap V [III] 59 [180])

ARTICLES VII AND VIII (IV). THE CHURCH

The Medieval Roman Catholic Church had developed a massive organizational structure for its operations, all revolving around the pope. The Lutherans insisted that the Church cannot be defined by its outward organization. The Church is instead defined as the gathering of God's people around Christ's Word and Sacraments.

ARTICLE IX. BAPTISM

The Confutation accepted the Augsburg Confession's teaching on Baptism. Melanchthon repeats the Lutheran rejection of certain errors that had emerged elsewhere during the Reformation concerning Baptism in general and the Baptism of infants in particular.

ARTICLE X. THE HOLY SUPPER

The Confutation approved the Augsburg Confession's statement on the Lord's Supper. Unlike some of the other protestant churches that emerged after the Reformation, Lutheranism maintains the biblical and historic Church doctrine that the Lord's Supper is the true body and blood of Christ.

ARTICLE XI. CONFESSION

The Confutation accepted the Augsburg Confession's statement about Confession, but insisted that the Church could order people to confess before a priest at least once a year. Melanchthon explains how in Lutheran churches the Sacraments are to be received often, but no laws are made about how often.

ARTICLE XIIa (V). REPENTANCE

The Confutation rejected the Lutheran teaching that penance, or repentance, consists only of contrition and faith. In this article, Melanchthon carefully demolishes terrible errors about how we are forgiven, including the Roman Catholic practice of selling indulgences.

> We say that contrition is the true terror of conscience, which feels that God is angry with sin and grieves that it has sinned. This contrition takes place when sins are condemned by God's Word. (Ap XIIa [V] 29)

As the second part of repentance we add faith in Christ. The Gospel, in which the forgiveness of sins is freely promised concerning Christ, should be presented to consciences in these terrors. They should believe that, for Christ's sake, their sins are freely forgiven. (Ap XIIa [V] 35)

ARTICLE XIIb (VI). CONFESSION AND SATISFACTION

The Roman Catholic Church transformed the great blessing of Confession and Absolution into a legalistic burden on the back of every Christian. Melanchthon makes it clear that Lutherans cherish private Confession and Absolution, not as a burden, but as God's forgiveness to relieve the believer burdened by sins.

ARTICLE XIII (VII). THE NUMBER AND USE OF THE SACRAMENTS

The Confutation demanded that Lutherans teach that there are exactly seven Sacraments. Melanchthon responded that if the Church chooses to consider the Sacraments as rites that God has commanded where grace is added, then there would be three: Baptism, the Lord's Supper, and Absolution or Repentance.

ARTICLE XIV. ORDER IN THE CHURCH

Here Melanchthon affirms Lutheranism's desire to maintain whatever best contributes to good order, peace, and harmony in the Church. Lutheranism has never insisted on one form of Church government over another, as do the Roman Catholic or Reformed churches.

ARTICLE XV (VIII). HUMAN TRADITIONS IN THE CHURCH

The Confutation accepted this article in some ways but opposed the Augsburg Confession's statement that Christians should reject any traditions created to appease God. Melanchthon argued that our praise and thanksgiving for God's gifts in worship are a response to His grace, not a condition for receiving it.

ARTICLE XVI. POLITICAL ORDER

The Augsburg Confession and Apology state very plainly that Lutherans support the role of government. Christians as individuals have the freedom and the duty to participate in proper political life. The Roman Catholic Church often improperly interfered with the rule of the government.

ARTICLE XVII. CHRIST'S RETURN FOR JUDGMENT

During the Reformation, radical groups made numerous predictions about the end of the world. These dangerous predictions still plague the Church today. The vast majority of Christians, however, agree on the important article of faith about the end times that is beautifully summarized in the Apostles' Creed.

ARTICLE XVIII. FREE WILL

This article is central to the Apology. Melanchthon exposes the Roman Catholic attitudes about a person's ability, under his own powers, to bring himself to love God. Instead, Melanchthon explains the biblical truth that people have free will in earthly matters (civil righteousness) but not in spiritual matters (spiritual righteousness).

> Civil righteousness is assigned to free will, and spiritual righteousness is assigned to the governing of the Holy Spirit in the reborn. In this way, outward discipline is kept, because all people should know that God requires this civil righteousness and that, to some extent, we can achieve it. And yet a distinction is shown between human and spiritual righteousness, between philosophical teaching and

the teaching of the Holy Spirit. . . . But those who dream that people can obey God's Law without the Holy Spirit, and that the Holy Spirit is given so that obeying the Law may be considered meritorious, have wickedly hindered the distinction. (Ap XVIII 75–76)

Article XIX. The Cause of Sin

The Confutation accepted the Augsburg Confession's teaching on the cause of sin. Both the Roman Catholics and the Lutherans agreed that, though God alone creates and preserves all nature, the cause of sin is the will of the devil and people turning away from God.

Article XX. Good Works

The Confutation rejected the Lutheran and biblical teaching that people do not earn the forgiveness of sins by good works. On this point, more so perhaps than on any other, Roman Catholic teaching is shown to be, at its essence, deeply against the Gospel.

Article XXI (IX). The Invocation of Saints

Melanchthon says that, in the end, all the Confutation did in its response to the Augsburg Confession's statement on praying to the saints was prove that the saints should be honored and that living saints may pray for others. Only the work of Christ, and not the good works or prayers of others, makes us right before God.

Article XXII (X). Both Kinds in the Lord's Supper

The Confutation rejected the Lutheran request that laypeople receive both the consecrated bread and wine in the Lord's Supper. In this article, Melanchthon opposes the Roman Catholic theologians and insists that there is no legitimate biblical reason to withhold the wine from the common people.

ARTICLE XXIII (XI). THE MARRIAGE OF PRIESTS

In this article, Melanchthon rebuts the Confutation's argument that priests should not marry. He bases his argument in the institution of marriage at creation. Marriage is a divine command for God's creation that the Church cannot refuse to pastors.

ARTICLE XXIV (XII). THE MASS

Melanchthon states that Lutherans keep all the primary forms of worship, or the Mass, that do not conflict with the Gospel. He defends the biblical teaching, contrary to the Roman Catholic teaching, that while we do receive Christ's true body and blood in the Sacrament, the priest does not re-sacrifice Christ each time the Mass is celebrated.

ARTICLE XXVII (XIII). MONASTIC VOWS

The Confutation, as could be expected, rejects the Augsburg Confession's position against monasticism as the highest calling of service to God. Lutheranism restored to the Church a proper understanding for how people can and do serve God in all the various callings in life.

ARTICLE XXVIII (XIV). CHURCH AUTHORITY

The issue in this article is whether Church leaders have the authority to command man-made regulations and impose them on people. Melanchthon argues that regulations must be in place to provide order and peace, but they must never suggest that anyone receives forgiveness from God by following them.

> We neither desire to desert truth necessary for the Church, nor can we agree with the adversaries in condemning it. For "we must obey God rather than

men." . . . This is our response to the Confutation. Now we leave it to the discernment of all the godly whether the adversaries are right in bragging that they have actually, from the Scriptures, refuted our Confession. (Ap XXVIII [XIV] 24–25, 26–27)

THE SMALCALD ARTICLES

The Smalcald Articles were written by Luther in late 1536. On June 4, 1536, Pope Paul III announced that a council would be held in the city of Mantua, Italy, in May 1537 to deal with the concerns of the Protestants. The elector (or prince) of Saxony asked Luther to prepare some articles for discussion at the council. Luther indicated on which points Lutherans would stand fast and on which points a compromise might be possible. These articles were never used for their intended purpose, but were instead presented at a meeting of Lutheran theologians in Smalcald, Germany, on February 7, 1537. Lutherans at once recognized their value as a statement of pure evangelical doctrine, and they were therefore included in the Book of Concord.

OUTLINE

Preface	IV. The Gospel
The First Part: Divine Majesty	V. Baptism
The Second Part: Office and Work of Jesus Christ	VI. The Sacrament of the Altar
I. The Chief Article	VII. The Keys
II. The Mass	VIII. Confession
The Invocation of Saints	IX. Excommunication
III. Chapters and Cloisters	X. Ordination and the Call
IV. The Papacy	XI. The Marriage of Priests
The Third Part	XII. The Church
I. Sin	XIII. How One Is Justified before God and Does Good Works
II. The Law	XIV. Monastic Vows
III. Repentance	XV. Human Traditions
The False Repentance of the Papists	

THE FIRST PART: DIVINE MAJESTY

Luther begins the articles by repeating the historic creeds and teachings that confess God the Holy Trinity and the two natures in Christ. He concludes by showing how these articles are the historic confession of the Christian Church upon which both Lutherans and Roman Catholics agree.

THE SECOND PART: OFFICE AND WORK OF JESUS CHRIST

ARTICLE I. THE CHIEF ARTICLE

After stating the things that Lutherans and Roman Catholics agree on, Luther launches immediately into the "chief article" of the Christian faith: Christ's saving work can never be given up, or compromised, for the sake of peace and unity in the Church.

ARTICLE II. THE MASS

Nowhere was Roman Catholicism's corruption of the doctrine of justification more clearly seen than in the abuses and errors associated with the celebration of Holy Communion. Luther forcefully calls the corruption of the Lord's Supper in the Roman Mass a "horrible abomination" because it thoroughly goes against the chief article of faith, justification.

ARTICLE III. CHAPTERS AND CLOISTERS

Reflecting on his own experiences as a monk, Luther rejects the Roman Catholic system of monastic life. By making monasticism a way of earning eternal life, Roman Catholicism contradicted the chief article of the Christian faith.

> Monastic chapters and cloisters were formerly founded with the good intention of educating learned men and virtuous women. . . . If these

institutions will not serve this purpose, it is better to abandon them or tear them down than have their blasphemous, humanly invented services regarded as something better than the ordinary Christian life and the offices and callings ordained by God. This too is contrary to the chief article on the redemption through Jesus Christ. (SA II III)

Article IV. The Papacy

Luther flatly asserts that the pope is the Antichrist, a statement that may sound outrageous to most modern ears. The Bishop of Rome is no more than a pastor of God's people in Rome and of all those who voluntarily attach themselves to him.

THE THIRD PART

Article I. Sin

The major point of this article is to make sure that original sin is clearly seen as the root cause of all sin. Roman Catholics teach that humans have an ability to grasp and respond to grace. This teaching goes against the Bible, as it denies our need for Christ's sacrificial death for our salvation.

Article II: The Law

The Roman Catholics had accepted the unbiblical teaching that a person could truly keep God's Law by means of his or her own abilities. The Lutheran Reformation restored the proper biblical understanding of the chief purpose of the Law: to reveal mankind's sin and drive people to seek salvation only in Christ.

ARTICLE III. REPENTANCE

Roman Catholic theologians held that God gives His grace to those who repent of their sins by doing as much as they can of their own free will to make up for their sins. Luther put forward the proper biblical teaching about repentance, which is the interplay between the Law and the Gospel.

ARTICLE IV. THE GOSPEL

Luther details how the Gospel comes to us: through the preached Word of forgiveness. God generously gives His gifts. He also provides the Gospel in other forms, including Holy Baptism, the Lord's Supper, and God's Word shared among Christians who support and comfort one another with the Word of Christ.

> God is superabundantly generous in His grace: First, through the spoken Word, by which the forgiveness of sins is preached in the whole world. This is the particular office of the Gospel. Second, through Baptism. Third, through the holy Sacrament of the Altar. Fourth, through the Power of the Keys. Also through the mutual conversation and consolation of brethren, "Where two or three are gathered" (Matthew 18:20) and other such verses. (SA III IV)

ARTICLE V. BAPTISM

Luther emphasizes that the power and promise of Holy Baptism are located entirely in the life-giving Word of mercy and grace. Therefore, he rejects any notion that the water by itself or the actions in the ritual have any spiritual power.

ARTICLE VI. THE SACRAMENT OF THE ALTAR

Luther asserts that the bread and wine are the body and blood of Christ. They are present, distributed, and received by all who commune. The Roman Catholic theory of transubstantiation is rejected. Instead, Lutherans take Scripture at face value, that Jesus' words are true.

> As for transubstantiation, we care nothing about the sophistic cunning by which they teach that bread and wine leave or lose their own natural substance so that only the appearance and color of bread remain, and not true bread. For it is in perfect agreement with Holy Scriptures that there is, and remains, bread, as Paul himself calls it, "The bread that we break" and "Let a person . . . so eat of the bread." (SA III VI 5)

ARTICLE VII. THE KEYS

Luther states that the authority to bind sins and not forgive them, or to loose sins by forgiving them, is a power entrusted by Christ to His Church, not just to the pope and religious leaders.

ARTICLE VIII. CONFESSION

Luther never intended to abolish private Confession and Absolution, only to do away with the errors and abuses that had come to be associated with it. Specifically, Luther rejected requiring people to list and name all their sins in confession and instead trust in the power of God's Word.

ARTICLE IX. EXCOMMUNICATION

Luther rejects any suggestion that the pope can ban people from both Church and society. However, Luther clearly does acknowledge biblical excommunication, that is, preventing openly unrepentant sinners from fellowship in the Church until they repent and turn from their sin.

ARTICLE X. ORDINATION AND THE CALL

Luther insists that the authority and right to ordain theologically and personally qualified men for the office of pastor is to be used within the Church. This power does not come from religious leaders or overseers but from the pastors and congregations.

ARTICLE XI. THE MARRIAGE OF PRIESTS

The fact that Roman Catholic priests were denied marriage under the pope is a clear indication of the anti-Christian nature of the office of the pope. Just as we cannot make a man a woman, or a woman a man, so the Church cannot forbid what God has created and ordained: marriage.

> They have neither the authority nor the right to ban marriage and to burden the divine order of priests with perpetual celibacy. They have acted like anti-Christian, tyrannical, desperate scoundrels, and by this have caused all kinds of horrible, outrageous, innumerable sins of unchastity. (SA III XI 1)

ARTICLE XII. THE CHURCH

The Church consists of those who hear and follow the voice of the Good Shepherd. The Church's holiness is not found in man-made rituals and decorations. It is found only in the Word of God, which creates and calls forth true faith in Christ.

> We do not agree with them [the Papists] that they are the Church. . . . Nor will we listen to those things that, under the name of Church, they command or forbid. Thank God, ‹today› a seven-year-old child

knows what the Church is, namely, the holy believers and lambs who hear the voice of their Shepherd. (SA III XII 1)

ARTICLE XIII. HOW ONE IS JUSTIFIED BEFORE GOD AND DOES GOOD WORKS

Luther asserts once more, very plainly, the doctrine of justification. Saving faith produces in us a harvest of good works. All is covered over in the mercy of Christ, including our sinful and flawed "good works." Works do not save; they are the fruit of salvation.

ARTICLE XIV. MONASTIC VOWS

As in the article on marriage, Luther is speaking here as a former monk. He states very plainly that monastic vows are, in fact, blasphemy against God.

> Since monastic vows directly conflict with the first chief article, they must be absolutely abolished. . . . He who makes a vow to live as a monk believes that he will enter upon a way of life holier than ordinary Christians lead. He wants to earn heaven by his own works, not only for himself, but also for others. This is to deny Christ. (SA III XIV)

ARTICLE XV. HUMAN TRADITIONS

Luther concludes his confession by rejecting any suggestion that human traditions produce the forgiveness of sins. For Luther, none of these teachings could be compromised. Finally, Luther firmly states that we should have nothing to do with superstitious Roman Catholic practices.

These are the articles on which I must stand, and, God willing, shall stand, even to my death. I do not know how to change or yield anything in them. If anyone wants to yield anything, let him do it at the peril of his conscience. (SA III XV 3)

THE TREATISE ON THE POWER AND PRIMACY OF THE POPE

The Treatise on the Power and Primacy of the Pope was prepared by Philip Melanchthon at the meeting at Smalcald in 1537. Luther's Smalcald Articles were to be discussed at the meeting, but, partly because Luther became ill, they were never publicly presented to the assembly. Instead, Melanchthon was requested to prepare a treatise, a kind of formal written statement. This treatise was intended to serve as a supplement to the Augsburg Confession, giving the Lutheran position on the pope, the leader of the Roman Catholic Church.

OUTLINE

[Introduction]	[A Contrast between Christ and the Pope]
[Testimony of Scripture]	[The Marks of the Antichrist]
Testimony of History	The Power and Jurisdiction of Bishops
[Refutation of Roman Arguments]	

[INTRODUCTION]

Melanchthon begins by stating the false beliefs of the Roman Catholic Church about the pope. Though these positions have changed and moderated over the years, the claim of papal supremacy above all other Christian pastors is still very much part of Roman Catholic doctrine.

> The Roman pontiff claims for himself that he is ‹supreme above› all bishops and pastors by divine right. Second, he adds that by divine right he has both swords, that is, the authority also to enthrone and depose kings ‹,regulate secular dominions, and such›. Third, he says that to believe this is necessary for salvation. For these reasons, the Roman bishop calls himself ‹and boasts that he is› the vicar of Christ on earth. These three articles we hold to be false, godless, tyrannical, and destructive to the Church. (Tr 1–4)

[TESTIMONY OF SCRIPTURE]

Melanchthon presents basic biblical texts refuting claims about the superiority of the pope. He clarifies how the authority of pastors does not flow from Peter's special position, as the Roman Catholics falsely believed. Instead, the authority of pastors comes from the Word of God.

TESTIMONY OF HISTORY

Besides Scripture, history also shows that the claims of the pope lack a foundation in the Church's practice through the ages. Melanchthon cites historical cases to show the development of the papacy over time, revealing it to be a human, not divine, position.

Therefore, it is clear enough that the churches did not then grant superiority and domination to the bishop of Rome. . . . Since the superiority the pope claims for himself is impossible and has not been acknowledged by churches in the greater part of the world, it is clear enough that it was not instituted ⟨by Christ and does not spring from divine law⟩. (Tr 15–16)

[REFUTATION OF ROMAN ARGUMENTS]

Melanchthon then deals clearly with the Bible verse most commonly used by the Roman Catholic Church to establish papal superiority: Matthew 16:18, the famous "you are Peter" passage. He shows how the ministry of the Word is founded not on a man, Peter, but upon his confession.

[A CONTRAST BETWEEN CHRIST AND THE POPE]

Melanchthon goes in-depth with his descriptions of how the pope is not the Christ.

[THE MARKS OF THE ANTICHRIST]

St. Paul prophesies in 2 Thessalonians 2:2–11 that a leader will take a seat in God's Church, insisting on false teachings and practices. The Lutheran Confessions call this person the "Antichrist" (based on 1 John 2:18). Because Scripture warns of his coming within the Church, the Confessions call the Roman Catholic pope Antichrist.

It is clear that the Roman pontiffs, with their followers, defend godless doctrines and godless services. And the marks of Antichrist plainly agree with the kingdom of the pope and his followers. For Paul, in describing Antichrist to the Thessalonians, calls him an enemy of Christ. . . . He calls him the enemy of Christ, because he will invent doctrine conflicting with the Gospel and will claim for himself divine authority. (Tr 39)

THE POWER AND JURISDICTION OF BISHOPS

This portion of the Treatise is one of the most important commentaries in the Book of Concord on the office and duties of pastors. In the Church, the power or authority of the ministry consists in preaching the Gospel, forgiving sins, administering the Sacraments, and excommunicating persons guilty of public sins.

ℬℐℂℬ

THE SMALL CATECHISM

Among the Lutheran Confessions, the two catechisms, or teaching handbooks, of Dr. Martin Luther are the earliest. Luther published them in the spring of 1529 to help pastors, teachers, and parents give instruction in the chief parts of Christian doctrine. The Small Catechism is a short work composed to educate the laity in the basics of the Christian faith. It was intended for the head of the household to use to teach the faith in each household.

OUTLINE

Preface	V. How the Unlearned Should Be Taught to Confess
I. The Ten Commandments	VI. The Sacrament of the Altar
II. The Creed	Daily Prayers
III. The Lord's Prayer	Table of Duties
IV. The Sacrament of Holy Baptism	

PREFACE

In his preface to the Small Catechism, Luther expresses his frustration over people abusing the freedom of the Gospel. He describes a process for teaching and learning to memorize and retain the central truths of the Christian faith contained in the Small Catechism.

> Therefore, I beg you all for God's sake, my dear sirs and brethren, who are pastors or preachers, to devote yourselves heartily to your office. Have pity on the people who are entrusted to you and help us teach the catechism to the people, and especially to the young. (SC Preface 6)

I. THE TEN COMMANDMENTS

The Ten Commandants are God's moral law, what is right and wrong for all people. Luther begins the Small Catechism by focusing on this teaching, not only showing God's good desires for His people, but also revealing our sin and disobedience and need for forgiveness.

II. THE CREED

The second main teaching, or chief part, is the Apostles' Creed. This historic confession of the Church summarizes what the Bible teaches about the triune God. Luther divides the Creed into three sections, adding explanation about each person of the Trinity.

III. THE LORD'S PRAYER

Prayer is talking to God in our thoughts and words. The third chief part of the Small Catechism focuses on learning to pray through the Lord's Prayer. This teaching flows naturally from the

Creed as it helps us understand what we are to pray for and how we are to live each day as God's redeemed children in Christ.

IV. THE SACRAMENT OF HOLY BAPTISM

After the first three chief parts, Luther then turns to what the Bible says about the Sacraments. These are the great mysteries of the faith where God attaches His Word to a physical element to deliver the forgiveness of sins. Baptism delivers God's forgiveness, at Jesus' command, through water and the Word.

V. HOW THE UNLEARNED SHOULD BE TAUGHT TO CONFESS

Luther then teaches on the authority Jesus gave to the Church to forgive and not forgive sins, called the Office of the Keys. Luther gives a model for how Christians can faithfully and properly confess their sins to their pastors and receive this forgiveness through the pastor's absolution, or announcement of forgiveness.

VI. THE SACRAMENT OF THE ALTAR

Likewise, using Scripture, Luther teaches on the Sacrament of the Altar, also known as the Lord's Supper or Communion. He simply and plainly explains how the Bible teaches that the bread and the wine is the body and blood of Christ, given for us for the forgiveness of sins.

DAILY PRAYERS

Near the end of the Small Catechism, Luther includes some models for daily prayers for morning and evening as well as at meal times. Luther taught that households should pray and gather around God's Word together at consistent times within the routines of daily life.

TABLE OF DUTIES

In this final section, Luther gives a list of Bible passages that show God's desire for how His people should live within their various responsibilities in life, or vocations. Having learned the fundamentals of the faith, Christians are encouraged by Luther to live faithful lives of love and service within their duties.

ಐಾಇ

The Large Catechism

The Large Catechism of 1529 is longer than the Small Catechism that Luther produced the same year. More than the Small Catechism, the Large Catechism was written to encourage and guide teachers of the faith. Though covering the same chief parts of Christian doctrine as the Small Catechism, the Large Catechism is really a series of re-edited sermons that Luther preached.

OUTLINE

Longer Preface	Part III. The Lord's Prayer
Shorter Preface	Part IV. Baptism
Part I. The Ten Commandments	Infant Baptism
Part II. The Apostles' Creed	Part V. The Sacrament of the Altar

PREFACE

In this preface, Luther focuses on the clergy's faults and failings. He chastises and rebukes lazy pastors who do as little as possible when it comes to preaching and teaching, and who are lax in their own personal prayer and meditation on God's Word.

> But for myself I say this: I am also a doctor and preacher; yes, as learned and experienced as all the people who have such assumptions and contentment. Yet I act as a child who is being taught the catechism. Every morning—and whenever I have time—I read and say, word for word, the Ten Commandments, the Creed, the Lord's Prayer, the Psalms, and such. I must still read and study them daily. Yet I cannot master the catechism as I wish. But I must remain a child and pupil of the catechism, and am glad to remain so. (LC Long Preface 7–8)

I. THE TEN COMMANDMENTS

Luther begins this handbook on teaching by focusing on God's moral law for all people in the Ten Commandments. Though God expects us to follow His commands, we cannot do so perfectly. The Commandments point us to our need for forgiveness in Jesus.

> Now we have the Ten Commandments, a summary of divine teaching about what we are to do in order that our whole life may be pleasing to God. Everything that is to be a good work must arise and flow from and in this true fountain and channel. So apart from the Ten Commandments no work or thing can

be good or pleasing to God, no matter how great or precious it is in the world's eyes. (LC I 311)

II. The Apostles' Creed

The Creed section contains extensive commentary on the Apostles' Creed, divided up into the three articles focused on the Father, Son, and Holy Spirit. The Ten Commandments show us what we are and are not to do, while the Creed shows us the One who creates, redeems, and sanctifies us.

> So far we have heard the first part of Christian doctrine. We have seen all that God wants us to do or not to do. Now there properly follows the Creed, which sets forth to us everything that we must expect and receive from God. To state it quite briefly, the Creed teaches us to know Him fully. (LC II 1)

III. The Lord's Prayer

Christ gave us the Lord's Prayer so that we will know both how to pray and for what to pray. In his catechisms, Luther advises the use of set forms and patterns of prayer and recommends devoting times throughout each day to pray the Lord's Prayer.

IV. Baptism

God's Word of Gospel-promise makes Baptism what it is, giving us a new identity in Christ. For Luther, Confession and Absolution are included under Baptism and the proclamation of the Gospel. True repentance is daily returning to Baptism.

V. The Sacrament of the Altar

When Jesus tells us the bread and wine are His body and blood, they are what He says. What we receive in the Sacrament of the Altar is a great "treasure": the forgiveness of sins. Luther urges Christians to receive the Sacrament frequently.

> In conclusion, since we now have the true understanding and doctrine of the Sacrament, there is also need for some admonition and encouragement. Then people may not let such a great treasure—daily administered and distributed among Christians—pass by unnoticed. So those who want to be Christians may prepare to receive this praiseworthy Sacrament often. (LC V 39)

THE FORMULA OF CONCORD

The Formula of Concord was written a generation after Luther's death. Serious controversies had arisen among theologians of the Augsburg Confession; these threatened the very life of the Reformation. The Formula of Concord deals with these dissensions and presents sound biblical doctrine on the disputed issues. The Formula of Concord is divided into two parts. The Solid Declaration is the unabridged version. The Epitome is an abridged version intended for congregations to study. The Epitome comes before the Solid Declaration in the order of documents in the Book of Concord.

OUTLINE

The Summary Content, Rule, and Norm	VII. The Holy Supper of Christ
I. Original Sin	VIII. The Person of Christ
II. Free Will, or Human Powers	IX. The Descent of Christ to Hell
III. The Righteousness of Faith before God	X. Church Practices
IV. Good Works	XI. God's Eternal Foreknowledge <Predestination> and Election
V. The Law and the Gospel	XII. Other Factions <Heresies> and Sects
VI. The Third Use of God's Law	

The Summary Content, Rule, and Norm

What is the sole source of doctrine in the Church? The Bible, and the Bible alone. Church creeds and confessions, however, function as witnesses to that truth. Today, in authentically Lutheran churches, pastors and other Church workers pledge to faithfully teach and practice according to the Scriptures and the Lutheran Confessions, just as they have done for nearly five hundred years.

Article I. Original Sin

Lutherans believe the biblical truth that sin is a very deep and complete corruption of our human nature. No one except Christ Jesus, our Lord, can overcome this corruption for us and save us from it. He brings us to new life through His Gospel in Word and Sacraments.

Article II. Free Will

While we are free to choose in earthly matters, we have no power, ability, or free will in spiritual matters. Before coming to faith, we are incapable of responding to or cooperating with God's grace. After coming to faith and because of Christ, the new man in us does in fact respond to and cooperate with God the Holy Spirit.

Article III. The Righteousness of Faith before God

We are justified by God's grace alone, through faith alone, which receives the righteousness of Christ. Our righteousness before God comes from God's gift of Christ's righteousness to us. Faith is the means, or instrument, by which we receive Christ's righteousness. Good works are the fruit of, not the cause of, that justifying faith.

It is unanimously confessed in our churches, in accordance with God's Word and the meaning of the Augsburg Confession, that we poor sinners are justified before God and saved alone through faith in Christ. Christ alone is our Righteousness, who is true God and man, because in Him the divine and human natures are personally united with each other (Jeremiah 23:6; 1 Corinthians 1:30; 2 Corinthians 5:21). (FC Ep III 1)

ARTICLE IV. GOOD WORKS

It is wrong to say that good works are necessary for salvation. It is also wrong to say that they are harmful for salvation. A person who is alive through faith in Christ will do good works. While good works play no role in our salvation, they are very much part of our lives as God's children.

ARTICLE V. THE LAW AND THE GOSPEL

This article provides a careful definition of the important terms *Law* and *Gospel*. Strictly speaking, the Gospel is entirely and only about the good news of our salvation in Christ: what He has done for us through His life, death, and resurrection. A person who claims that the Gospel is about what we are to do confuses both Law and Gospel.

> The distinction between the Law and the Gospel is a particularly brilliant light. It serves the purpose of rightly dividing God's Word and properly explaining and understanding the Scriptures of the holy prophets and apostles. We must guard this distinction with special care, so that these two doctrines may not be mixed with each other, or a law

be made out of the Gospel. When that happens, Christ's merit is hidden and troubled consciences are robbed of comfort, which they otherwise have in the Holy Gospel when it is preached genuinely and purely. For by the Gospel they can support themselves in their most difficult trials against the Law's terrors. (FC SD V 1)

ARTICLE VI. THE THIRD USE OF GOD'S LAW

God uses His Law in three ways: to maintain external discipline in society (like a curb), to lead us to recognize our sin (like a mirror), and to guide Christians so that they will know what is pleasing to Him (like a rule). Because the old sinful flesh clings to us until we die, we Christians need the Law as a guide for works that are pleasing to God and are appointed by God for us to do.

> God's Law is useful (1) because external discipline and decency are maintained by it against wild, disobedient people; (2) likewise, through the Law people are brought to a knowledge of their sins; and also, (3) when people have been born anew by God's Spirit, converted to the Lord, and Moses's veil has been lifted from them, they live and walk in the Law. (FC SD VI 1)

ARTICLE VII. THE HOLY SUPPER OF CHRIST

On the basis of the Word and promise of Christ, Lutherans believe that the true body and true blood of Jesus are actually present, distributed, and orally received in Holy Communion. The authors of the Formula of Concord defend the truth against the congregations of the Reformed tradition, who believe in only a symbolic or spiritual presence.

> Question: In the Holy Supper, are the true body and blood of our Lord Jesus Christ (a) truly and essentially present, (b) distributed with the bread and wine, and (c) received with the mouth by all those who use this Sacrament—whether they are worthy or unworthy, godly or ungodly, believing or unbelieving? Are they received by the believing for consolation and life, but by the unbelieving for judgment? The Sacramentarians say No. We say Yes. (FC Ep VII 2)

Article VIII. The Person of Christ

Many objections to the Lutheran doctrine of the Lord's Supper are based on incomplete understandings concerning the relationship of Christ's divine and human natures. The writers of the Formula of Concord defended how the doctrine of the incarnation—Christ the Son of God taking on human flesh—is a powerful comfort and treasure for Christians receiving the Lord's Supper.

Article IX. The Descent of Christ to Hell

This article sought to put an end to the squabbling that had arisen among Lutherans over the meaning of Christ's descent to hell, as confessed in the Creed. The writers of the Formula of Concord based their conclusions on one of Luther's sermons discussing this issue.

Article X. Church Practices

This article addresses matters that Scripture neither commands nor forbids. Keeping or omitting certain Church practices can be an obstacle and offense to the Gospel and may even lead to false teaching. The article contains a key insight that agreement in doctrine and all its articles is necessary for Church fellowship, not complete unity in practice.

ARTICLE XI. GOD'S ETERNAL FOREKNOWLEDGE <PREDESTINATION> AND ELECTION

Although this article was not written in response to a specific controversy among Lutherans, it was wisely included. John Calvin and his followers had developed a teaching commonly known as "double predestination." This article clearly dismantles this dreadful and nonbiblical teaching and exposes it as a great error.

> If we want to think or speak correctly and usefully about eternal election, or the predestination or preordination of God's children to eternal life, we should make it our custom to avoid speculating about God's bare, secret, concealed, mysterious foreknowledge. Instead, we should think or speak about how God's counsel, purpose, and ordination in Christ Jesus—who is the true Book of Life—is revealed to us through the Word. In other words, the entire teaching about God's purpose, counsel, will, and ordination belongs to our redemption, call, justification, and salvation. (FC SD XI 13–14)

ARTICLE XII. OTHER FACTIONS <HERESIES> AND SECTS

This article lists and condemns a host of false teachings, and the groups promoting them, as potentially damning. Modern errors, false teachings, and heresies are merely recycled from the past and repackaged with attractive gimmicks.

ဆာ‌ငာ

For Further Reading

This booklet is only a simple summary of the historical context and teachings of the Book of Concord. We encourage you now to extend your learning by reading the Book of Concord yourself. The resource we recommend, that was used in the development of this book, is *Concordia: The Lutheran Confessions; A Reader's Edition of the Book of Concord*, second edition (CPH, 2006). It includes not only the text of the Book of Concord but also a wealth of introductory information, Scripture references, historical information, and images to help enrich your personal study.

If you'd like to read more about the doctrines, events, and people involved in the Book of Concord, here are suggestions for other Concordia Publishing House books for further study:

- *The Augsburg Confession: A Collection of Sources with a Historical Introduction* by Johann Michael Reu

- *The Confessional Principle and the Confessions of the Lutheran Church* by Theodore E. Schmauk and C. Theodore Benze

- *A Contemporary Look at the Formula of Concord*, edited by Robert D. Preus and Wilbert H. Rosin

- *The Doctrine of Faith: A Study of the Augsburg Confession and Contemporary Ecumenical Documents* by Nestor Beck

- *Frederick the Wise: Seen and Unseen Lives of Martin Luther's Protector* by Sam Wellman

- *Getting into the Theology of Concord: A Study of the Book of Concord* by Robert D. Preus

- *Historical Introductions to the Lutheran Confessions: As Contained in the Book of Concord in 1580* by F. Bente

- *John Frederick the Magnanimous: Defender of Martin Luther and Hero of the Reformation*, compiled by Dr. Georg Mentz; translated by James Langebartels

- *The Lutheran Difference: An Explanation and Comparison of Christian Beliefs*, edited by Edward A. Engelbrecht

- *Nikolaus von Amsdorf: Champion of Martin Luther's Reformation* by Robert Kolb

- *Philipp of Hesse: Unlikely Hero of the Reformation* by John E. Helmke

- *The Protestant Reformation: 1517–1559* by Lewis W. Spitz

- *The Reformation* by Cameron A. MacKenzie

- *The Second Martin: The Life and Theology of Martin Chemnitz* by Jacob A. O. Preus

- *Tyranny and Resistance: The Magdeburg Confession and the Lutheran Tradition* by David Mark Whitford

- *We Confess Anthology* by Hermann Sasse; translated by Norman E. Nagel